BOOKS BY VICTOR HERNÁNDEZ CRUZ

Snaps
Mainland

MAINLAND

MAINLAND

POEMS BY
Victor Hernández Cruz

RANDOM HOUSE / NEW YORK

Library of Congress Cataloging in Publication Data

Cruz, Victor Hernández, 1949–
Mainland.
Poems.
I. Title.
PS3553.R8M3   811'.5'4   72–10662
ISBN 0–394–46091–X (hardbound)
ISBN 0–394–70619–6 (paperbound)

MANUFACTURED IN THE UNITED STATES OF AMERICA

FIRST EDITION

"African Things" from *Negro Digest,* November, 1969. Copyright
© 1969 by *Negro Digest.* Reprinted by permission of *Black World*
and the author.

"En La Casa de Verta" from *Vibration Cooking* by Verta Mae.
Copyright © 1970 by Verta Grosvenor. Reprinted by permission
of Doubleday & Company, Inc.

"The Sounds of Colors" from *Confrontations,* Volume I, Number
II, 1971.

"Feast of the Guardian Saint" will appear in a forthcoming issue
of *Mundus Artium.*

Para mi mama Rosa-Julia
y mi sister Gladys
Estos Poemas

"A veces, de sus roncos altamares ocultos, de esas inexploradas distancias, vienen ecos tan vagos, que se pierden como ondas desmayadas sobre una playa inmóvil de bruma y de silencio. Son mensajes que llegan desesperadamente del ignorado fondo de estos dramas secretos: gritos de auxilio, voces de socorro, gemidos, cual de un navío enorme que naufraga a lo lejos."

Luis Palés Matos

"Sometimes, from its hidden hoarse-voiced high sea, from those unexplored distances, come echoes so vague that they lose themselves like swooning waves on an immobile coast of mists and silence. They are messages that reach us in desperation from the unknown depths of these secret dramas; cries for help, voices, moans like those from a huge ship that is being wrecked in the distance."

Luis Palés Matos

CONTENTS

III/BORINKEN

Rhythm Section
Part One

You Gotta Have Your Tips On Fire

You never know who has your memory
in their drinks
In the cities that move into other
cities
Into other times
Ancient cities
You never know who wants to throw
you into that timeless space
Where you forget your name
And the face of the woman you love
Camara
You gotta have your tips on fire
You never know who has your thoughts
locked up in some small room
Wishing a thousand storms would
hit your doorway
Wishing you whirlwinds for paths
and hurricanes for the mornings
that open your days
You gotta have your tips on fire
Pana
Because they make doors out of pure
space
And you have to swing them open
So they know
You are around the wind
You are in the wind with your own
dance
You never know who stabs your
shadow full of holes

You gotta have your tips on fire
You never will be in the wrong place
For the universe will feel your heat
And arrange its dance on your head
There will be a Sun/Risa
On your lips
But
You gotta have your tips on fire
Carnal.

#1   Atmosphere

Don Arturo says:
You have to know
what the atmosphere
is creating
You have to know
Because if it's good
You can go somewhere
and make your own.

#2   Memory

Don Arturo says:
You have to know
what you once said
Because it could
travel in the air
for years
And return in different
clothes
And then you have to
buy it.

#3 Business

Don Arturo says:
There was a man
who sold puppets and whistles
for a living
He also played guitar
He used to go
to the shopping areas
and draw huge crowds
They bought his whistles
and puppets
They threw money into
his guitar
This was against the law
So he was arrested at
least three times a week
When his turn came up
in the courtroom
He took a puppet out
and put a show on
All the detectives
and court clerks
rolled on the floor
When he finished
they all bought puppets
and whistles from him
The judge got angry
and yelled:
What kind of business
is this
And the man said

I am the monkey man
and the
Monkey man sells
Monkey business.

#4   Love

Don Arturo says:
If you put your hands
in all the time
Some day it will fly
away with your mind

#5   Music

Don Arturo says:
There's supposed to
be more sauce than
fish
It suppose to be
like riding on a
horse
or stepping out
of the room
Without a single
motion.

Thursday

Water is Manhattan
The trains and the buses they sail
Stores and the lights
In the water wet
Thursday far and near strange
A dream Thursday and island
There are two in the memory

What forces elevated me today
To look for what I need
This corner of this earth
Searching for a way to know you
Venus
Thursday Jupiter
Land of somebody's fathers

Wet lines between us all
as the city is bombarded by rain
Young as you are
Young as I am   young as the world
Young History

Now we open doors
Now we remember continents and how they
Danced under the water
Under the ground

Was it Thursday
Was it Thursday

Let me look at you Thursday
Let me look all inside your secret
Open your arms
Elevate
Like rising music
Like that music
that I love so much

Like that Spanish that you like to talk
Like the way you walk

I hold Thursday all in my arms
In the deep tunnel I hear your hair
As it brushes against your neck
As you move
As a dance
Coming to see what it is all about

I build bridges in the sky
Send waves of thoughts
Do you hear them?

Today I eat guineo
With my hands
Under a palm tree by the beach
Where I am not
Do you see the dance that could begin
Evolve.

Los New Yorks

In the news that sails through the air
Like the shaking seeds of maracas
I find you out

Suena

You don't have to move here
Just stand on the corner
Everything will pass you by
Like a merry-go-round the red
bricks will swing past your eyes
They will melt
So   old
will move out by themselves

Suena

I present you the tall skyscrapers
as merely huge palm trees with lights

Suena

The roaring of the trains is a fast
guaguanco
dance of the ages

Suena

Snow falls
Coconut chips galore

Take the train to Caguas
and the bus is only ten cents
to Aguas Buenas

Suena

A tropical wave settled here
And it is pulling the sun
with a romp
No one knows what to do

Suena

I am going home now
I am settled there with my fruits
Everything tastes good today
Even the ones that are grown here
Taste like they're from outer space
Walk y Suena
Do it strange
Los New Yorks.

BronxOmania

snake horse stops at bronx clouds
end of lines and tall windowed cement
comes to unpaved roads and wilderness
where the city is far
and spanish bakeries sell hot bread
the roar of the iron snake
plunges at closing doorways
down fifty blocks
is the island of Puerto Rico.

Coka-Moon (21st floor Water Street)

I look up at the rays
see the strength shaking up
the whole empire

Below the river boats
go by in slow breeze
the trucks load
boxes of cans

The island of commerce is
bending round the edge
by the bridge
to the industrial smack
of the planet

Where you can see it

The trains chu-chu in on the water
ride slowly without their wheels
green tugboats
their bodies surrounded by rubber
smashing sides against cargo ships

Brooklyn employment force
selling east river heroin
and busting heads in dice games
never going home to open their
arms to the eagles that land
on their windows

Where you can see it

At the bottom of the river
great musicians invent their
last solos
local newspaper reporters
dead from thirty years ago—
their bones dancing with some
river plants

In god we trust 1952 quarters
rest at the very bottom
flung there by bad luck fingers
looking for the blessings of all
good spirits

Where you can see it

Waterfront adventure
squeezing in on the belly
of Manhattan

Water gods dance out of the river
they fly and reach restful
colorful days of peace

In the paradise room
21 stories high up in the air
guarding the city
watching the 12 moons shine
down on the water.

To Dotty Gonzalez and her two Roots

Fourteenth Street
a million stories in one head/
in one day of daylight
saw her and her little black curls pushing
from her head/she reminded me of years ago
the park full of orange rock wine/walking
with her curly black hair just saying: how
you doing/tales O parading in the shit/O you
know you still looking sweet/he   she   she
he/together stories longer than the planet/
sweet honey coming from the cement corner/
we move to the side of rainbows and sit on the
chapters/thrilling sayings/listen a million
rivers away and she is still full of curls/
her skin blown to the right dimension/she speaks
and turns her face to the coming sky/we remember
chasing sounds from windows in quiet creeping
noches in back worlds to all/she held her two
new stories by their hands/they were born years
ago/both in nice warm summers going/she walked
into the future/her legs miles of soft muscle/
she feels her way to the store and spreads cheeks
and continues on/Fourteenth Street
a million stories in one head.

Notas #3

Amid
the air
legs slide from the runway
powerful mambo
mambo flares into hurricanes
of trumpets
sweet coco chips raining
drum sticks beat the skin
to crying
tears of guaracha
hands feeling hips of
the waves
mambo lost long
time ago
among the
talking moves of dancers
amid the
air

The Piano That Falls Asleep

Horizontal
light viewing from behind
shot up straight

Spider webs will never
survive between those
fingers

that swift move-
ment and when
in time the bone
connections are
forgotten

And they begin to
perform miracles
like attracting
thousands to come
by the harbor

Where in a room
full of instruments
Off the water
and the fish lives
Upon that piano
up front in
sight

Hands just lean back
to imaginary pillows

notes
merging up
like a gathering
of crazy mixed
up dreams.

Rhythm-Section-Part-One

A hundred miles of living rooms
with paintings on the walls
Throughout rhythm
Make one lovely ball
Place it in your mind
Dance
One thousand corners
All holding one million beats
Riding to a palace unknown
down the street
With eyes up ahead checking breaks
Taking slow steps to long section days

One million doors
leading no place in particular
with names as strange as
Mambo Julia and Sako Legs
printed by the side walls
Opening doors to blue edges
Somewhere stereo sky way
flaring zone ears

Orange Moona Beer
Coming
Juke
Flute
Pacheco stirs Oquendo
Daylight rumba
Greetings from the walls
You can walk right in

A dozen bridges
Yellow sparks from surface
The painting
goes out the door by itself
Eyes run up and down its legs

A million miles of lips kissing
Only they know where
Part-One is sabroso

Matilda stretches for miles
on her green covered
pink walled chamber of Z's
A thousand lights turn
electric wave blankets
Guaracha

Taking slow steps to long section days
Part-Two with a million stairs to climb

Dotted island in between library
and unseen park
Send messages for rhythm
Section-Part-One

Evoke the sounds
and spill through
the sky way
for the total zone.

Rhythm-Section-Part-Three

Ana
falls out of the meteorite
reading a maroon velvet book
her eyes x-ray the pages
which move by themselves
to unseen juke boxes
somewhere from a mountainous
window
her tickling head roars
sweet poems.

En La Casa De Verta

FOR VERTA MAE GROSVENOR

for on monday in 1969   on the streets
was diamonds   downtown society
bodegas one right after the other
avocado and tomato juice   space
ships parked in front of Vertas house
sparkling yellow metal   with stickers
from Venus Airlines   Moon Shuttle
Jupiter Car Service   Mars Heliport
and all on Monday by a bridge   1969
year of the Rooster   hot sauce
street beans
caribbean rice on the fire
with african juice   warming
the centuries and centuries
of sea exploration and mixing

here we all are in Vertas
soul space kitchen
taking off

Blue Boat

People walking down the street
like they're on their way to the clouds
or somewhere higher
Walking in silence
I listen to a thousand windows
lift themselves open
Out comes a million rhythmic
songs
Out comes a cup of water
Perhaps a mirror broke
Or someone is cleaning the house
Why in January cold you look
toward God's house with burning eyes
Why in July you skip in the street
In a light dress covering your knees
and your wind is like an elephant's
When one turns to look at the storm
All they see is you dancing by
Just a little bit.

And this is just a fragment of this
Massive day
And it is still early
and most of the noise is not here yet
All of you
What it is today
that I go out and can't help
but laugh every time I take three steps
There is always something popping
from the mad

Why is it that you walk down
the street like you're going to heaven
on a blue boat
On a blue boat full of songs
On a blue boat full of heads
leaning comfortably back
With a mambo that has a thousand trumpets
and 400 timbales
It is the secret guide of the navigator
Who sits in his room in the blue boat
The blue boat that is this day.

Discovery

Watching a thousand smiles
that were full of sadness
standing in a wall
all sideways
My ears are the walls
No one can see me there
I am quiet
Still
Like the owls who sit atop
telephone polls

The traffic between
the walls
Those smiles that come
and go
Those darkened whiskers
suspended in the air
Those souls
Spirits
Coming from one thing
and going to another
but belonging nowhere

The walls breathe
My ears are hung like
blankets
My legs disappear into the
roof
My hands touch the building
next door

I swing from the walls
to the ceilings
No one hears me

I watch a yellow dress
that floats across
the rooms and stares
out of the windows
The Saints walk through
the walls
San Martin has a whole bowl
of grapes sitting on
the altar
he eats one every time
he walks by

Words come out of the rooms
like millions of fire crackers
They slam
Dance against the walls

On a clear Jupiter
The sun enters
Works its way in
Through the parted curtains
It moves inside the yellow
dress that hangs on
Yolanda

So
If you see a yellow dress
flying
Looking down on those

who walk the earth
with borrowed shoes
It's only Yolanda
cooking food
In through the door
and out through
the roof

My ears are the walls
And they hear it all
The yellow dress
It sometimes slips
and falls
Way in there
Where a smile
is six hundred miles
Way in there
where the Indians went to/

Sueño

A Tito Rodriquez mambo somewhere in the
deep background of parties
Six shots in the middle of the night
They drown out the softball players'
argument
What it is
Six blasts of thunder
Shots are not the way you hear love
approaching your midnight bed
Six blasts and the shuffling of bodies
and feet
Ay Dios mío
God is suddenly ours
He is suddenly in the beer cans
and jumping from the uncut cake
Ay Dios mío
God is at the doorway standing
Entering
Noise of legs jumping on the
black and white marble stairs
Softball players with their
numbers on their caps
Reaching for the half-blue half-
beige walls
That turn into green screams
at the bottom
where the mailboxes sit opened

And two eyes jump from a window
To the iceman below

Who pours syrup into the paper
cups
That look like upside down pyramids
with red lines at the top
He sells it to little girls
who roll their pants up so that
their orange socks are in view
Style of the day
". . . if they are properly rolled
         you will never be late . . ."
Six gun shots come running out of the
building
And the iceman screams:
Got six more flavors
no one has ever tasted
Only in dreams.

Caminando

Take your moon face away
into the mountains of so many cities
and stare down
The invisible dance
over the cemetery of spirits
and spirits talk
La noche ojos grande
Green alleys to the future
Ways to the magic cave
You split in the spring wind
You have the key to all the doors
Be strong
Eat fish
Drink rum.

Flight

Berkeley/Over

1

Bird wings over the bay
Electronic bombs below
Waves talking to la moon
A town of philosophical habits
Cold turkey would kill it
So it just sits and cops
Everyday.

2

An empire of hidden houses
Behind the green wall of the hills
Staring down into the flats
Eyes looking for the airport
Where are the birds?

3

In the University a parade of sounds
Light show Music and Gowns
Talking walking
One day
When the sun came after the rain
Burgundy Almadén
A bit for San Pedro
The rest for the music.

4

The place had grown many
Creators from across the land
Some sit high up on the sides

33

of hills
Others walk miles just to visit.

5

When the Monsoon came
And some found nothing to do
But stare at candles
The house on Grove Street
Was the secret meeting place
For those who wanted to hear
the rhythms
Pure.

The Ways in San Francisco

Part One

Cross the metal into San Francisco
Round ball   seven hills
Painter's huge room
Elevator for 1000 pounds

In the mission I found Roberto V.
We slid down hills
Carro colorado swings up paved
mountains
Mexican frijoles and flour tortillas
Lick our fingernails clean
Call the lady and tell her to bring
some more
Esta Bueno
Cross the metal legs
hopping in the East Bay
wet pile
Cemento boxes hurl themselves
at passing white clouds
Cross metal legs
State College waves
far away hour of journey
Travelers breathe their peculiar
fumes into each other's teeth
Cross the metal link into the
Mission
With a straw hat and an unlit
cigar in a hidden pocket

no one knows
Roberto V. is San Francisco
He's got it in his
leather vest pocket
He is haunted by
architects and city planners
Where have you hidden the
streets of the Mission?

The stage coach goes on
the two thin rails
Across the metal esta Mexico
and
Malta India performing in
store windows

Market Street is the 42nd
street of the West
Morning men hold their heads
from hitting the floor of
the city
Cross metal links into
San Francisco

Words come out of car mufflers
as they fight for the finish
line
To cross the bridge in biting
delight
Roberto Vargas buys some tacos
and tortillas
He doesn't talk or giggle

The train bus holds hands with
wires
No one knows where they came
from
Wire lines all over the town
distract the sky
The train cha chas on two
straight lines

Cross metal links into
San Francisco
When the weather is fine
and there is plenty of time

Part Three

PARA ROBERTO VARGAS

Red falcon/4 in the morning
5 in the morning
daylight whistles
and R.V. driving his car
down San Fra himalayas
his eyes bouncing around
the corners for somewhere
to go

We join the feast in colorful
three massive rooms
somewhere on a deserted street
blown hippy tits stand against
walls
science pictures splashed against
floor and ceiling
a little dot show
nervous fingers change slides
and press down the switch
of many bulbs

We notice the air changes colors
We move into other rooms
way back in a closet full of sofas
An international conference is held
Ruben Dario comes by way of R.V.
fingernails as he pointed to a fact
that ran out of the building
It became lies and poems

38

short stories sneaking from the
room next door
We picked up and dragged ourselves
to the red rolls royce parked
horizontal on a one way street

We turned spiral hills
maneuvers guided by forces
outside the red coach
R.V. smiling and singing
louder than the coming earthquake
When it was very early
We ate under the silver sky
of Ruben Dario's parlors

Part Four

on 22nd and folsom
pacific ocean fish   boiling
far away and getting farther
a mean ice breeze sneaks upon
the city   makes everyone
speed up
when there is nothing to do
and the walls of the top floor
half a house no longer can
hold an urge to fly somewhere
and when lips have been pressed
together for three nights
walking around   studying hills
and wondering what 3,000 miles
away is like   after turning
down folsom of this west coast
city   head for the bay
looking for some loud beings
to show on the screen
at the edge of the nation
counting back on the population
and rows of homes   asleep
standing on the   last breath
of the town action
the moon   she comes down
and spreads her
legs wide.

California #2

In the hour of Fresno
A strong blue
Yellow god
Valley of no rain
Afternoon walks
Full of wind from the
tips of the hills

Gypsy sings a song
And we walk toward
the car
And travel to the secret
two room dwelling
To laugh and sleep
on the floor

The Hispanic morning
of Aztlan
Welcomed with Café
con Canela.

painting   #4
The aztec sun
is warm
round eyes that
sparkle
quiet lips
deeply behind a painted
face.

painting   #5
Purple orange blue
yellow walls
shooting shapes of
other worlds
geometric moons/spin
around its mysterious
creator.

The Sounds of Colors

FOR JOE OVERSTREET

painting #1
Go into
stars/the bluest
night in the world
the message loud & clear
red on purple
loud people of the
streets
turning into walls
as Chinese rockets
explode.

painting #2
Brown & blue waves
of nature
floating ladies
laughing gringo boredom
above
butterflies that throw
bombs and Missiles
happy holiday
on canvas bright.

painting #3
By the window
the owl sits in
yellow awareness
Filled with blackness
& love.

from the Secrets I

What did the astronauts speak
When they rode the eagle's neck?

We know but will not tell
Silly how you move thousands
of years/to walk down Bronx
Avenues with tight red pants
And a smile as wide as the trucks
That pass you by

Thoughts in Spanish run through
the mind
The buildings speak broken English

Aquí
Where the birds landed
Drinking water from the streams
Cortez not knowing the sound of lips
That paraded up and down the hemisphere
Began the hunt of all these years

We know/but only know
In warm July somewhere dancing
Out from our eyes

Aquí

Land of tall cylinders   glass
between cement shining
Land of forgotten tongues

That surface from time to time
once on the Lexington Avenue local
moving into 103rd street
We meet Caquax sitting waiting for
the express   we turn to say hello
But he has gone into the wall
Bronx of walking streets
That turn into large strong eagles
The astronauts dance la plena
They dance till dawn/and fly all
day

Walking down Bronx Avenues
In red high yellow legs
Suddenly you forget where you are

And what time is it?

from the Secrets II

This morning I move like the river
moves
Science in your eyes
Says the music elevates
past clouds
Some tall legs
encircle the river
Heads bob to the ticking
of the solar calendar
Do you remember
the fourth floor of the pyramids
The hilarious perfume of your
feathers
The soft music of the sea flute
This morning I move like the river
moves
In and out of rooms like the warm
wind passing through.

Interstate 80

Boola got off
in Salt Lake City
to sink down to
the town of Spanish Fork
and look for a treasure
left by a cousin of
Montezuma way
back when Columbus
knelt in front of
Isabel and sobbed
tears all over
her toenails

M.R. Fitz was heading
for Boston
and her long skinny
legs spread and
photographed the
driver/he wanted a
side pose

a gentleman fell off his
strong two feet   his
1956 Fabian wig flew
to the side

From Oakland to Chicago
Brian O'Toole a Mayflower
special citizen/hit the
bus toilet 87 times

we counted

Three pairs of Sun Glasses
from Reno to Omaha were
melted by el Sol/the
teacher of the moon & the Ocean

Olando S.
saw an ancestor of his in
some Mountains in
Colorado and got off
the bus.   I am sorry
but he was overwhelmed
and could not be stopped
he said he would contact you
after the eclipse

An old brother man
he spoke about losing
his teeth near San
Diego in a fight with
a gringo who tried to
stop him from entering
he never went back
he told of a woman
he slept on every night
she is there/y mi hija
también.

I'm from Denver
she said . . . soy buena
con la gente/my children
will grow into the sky

and shine again

mira/rainbow dance
baila/tu rainbow line
line all shades/mira rain-
bow line to mexico/to mexico
rainbow line . . . dance baila
y dice/dance baila y dice
en el sky rainbow line
point and see . . . mira rain-
bow colores en el cielo
mira rainbow colores en el cielo
dancing up ahead . . . mira bailando
como es/seven colors pass your
head/mira rainbow dance/bus
follows clouds on top
of rainbow dance/mira así es
mira así es . . . rainbow dance
to México from ice up north
to México/el rainbow dance
seven colors chasing each
other cross the land air
mira baila con the rainbow
walk on the red/to México
walk on the red to México
walk on the red to Jalisco
and dance/mira baila con eso
que bueno esta/in seven colors
the rainbow ahead/put your
eyes in the blue mirror of
sun glasses and the window
will disappear/produce a
vision as long as days

Nebraska

La luna
Sang the miles por los palos
de Nebraska
You bunch of lights
And houses   How did you walk
to this place
Buffalo Bill
Better know him some Spanish
Para Horses   ride
rubber horseshoes
moderno.

El café
Boiled water /no milk in sight.
Homes that will travel interstate
80 tomorrow in the morning
for the next edge of town.

The cowgirls / the local rodeo
As they galloped by their hair
unmoved by 15 miles per hour wind
It seems that 25 pounds of hair spray
is enough to hold a mountain down
Their hair style longer than their
faces.
Que Pasa?
Y los palos
do not feel at home any more
La luna
goes round the star dotted cielo

Let's watch
In this part of Mexico
Se habla inglish.

Chicago/3 Hours

State Street's cold mingling
crowds of Christmas
The town of garages and lonely
alleys
Traffic chaos—
That melody of a fast moving
civilization
Part cowboy   Part Anglo
For the famous breeze
Bacardi light
Chicago the first apple
for a long long time
Night and theater lights
Night and the river shows waves
A spirit walks the bridge with
cement still tied to his legs
Smoke is wind/in the wind

Someone told me el hijo de Cortijo
is somewhere in this town
Ay le lo li le lo li
That's enough to keep you warm
Say it one more time
Ay le lo li le lo li.

Entering Detroit

Detroit popped in the window
when my eyes opened/smoke coming
out of its head
headlights writing poems
on dirty floors/the bus window is light
blue/I never saw a city like that
popping at the end of dreams from
hard plastic cushioned red seats/
cement road connecting
nation/get off and refuel and start
the ride again/Detroit becomes part
of the road we passed six hours ago
writing in the shadow of Lake Erie
loud natural force

(on the other side of 4th of july calendar mark)

Las Vegas

In the brown Nevada desert
are your light bulbs
City of coins
George Washington and Lincoln
Slide into the slot machines
You are the stranger
That is too common
In the middle of nowhere
The poor middle aged men
Lose their hair
At the tables
Otherwise they'd have
Nothing to do.

Poem

The greater cities are
surrounded by woods
Jungles secretly
of America

Behind lights
the green
Green eyes of Tree gods
Rhythm we would call it Puerto Rico
But it doesn't begin to be as real

Silver of the moon
On the upper Hudson
Green Quiet night
Night island wish
Outside the stars
get fatter and louder
Secret jungle where
the moon is closer
Highway to the skies
Secret
Outside getting cold
We talk to the wind
That moves the world
before it becomes foul
Over the heads of
the buildings

We take it in our mouths
Drunk outside great

Electrical Apple / Nueva York
No Puerto Rico
Nueva York
No Puerto Rico/

Borinken

Poem

Your head it waves outside
You are as deep and heavy as the ocean
Night and day
Cabo Rojo   the stars
Day and night
Arecibo   music in green
It rains   Rain washes coconuts
The mangos they fall off the trees
In midnights   You hear them falling
Sunshine   sol
Your eyes they become one with the light
It is early   Early Early Early
And the rooster is early
Like a natural alarm
The music of the morning

Your head is full of the ocean and
The mystery of the sea shells
It moves like the waves

Moving outside the rhythms of life
Dawn birth deep in the mountains
Your eyes   they move
In and out of the woods
They look for spirits

Here is where our mothers are from
From this land sitting
All pregnant with sweetness
And trees that want to be the wind

Walking through the little space
The trees make
You want to laugh
In this lonely night there is music
And you do
And you don't stop
And the music is right behind you

Coquí   Coquí   Coquí   Coquí

Here is where the journey started
And you laugh as tall as palm trees
And you taste as good as pasteles
You dance toward the silver of the stars
Everything moves with you
Like a tropical train.

Feast of The Guardian Saint

As if from the top
of mountains
Came voices
to modern wise men
Parading in a circus-
like fiesta
In the plaza of Cieba
Puerto Rico

Who are the people
wrapped in cloth
With their blue bell bottoms
and the señoritas with their
beige hot pants
Cieba from all the homes
that line your streets
Poured this mass of bodies
They put all their fires
on
All the colors for tonight
the height of la fiesta
of your guardian saint
All the colors for him
for he has watched well
over the mountains

Afternoons drive into nights
The machines turn
For twenty five cents
your body could go round

in circles for 8 minutes
Surrounded by multi-colored
light bulbs that go on and off
As the ride dips
low to the earth
and swings to the three
early stars
Shoots into space in circles
Spinning like the spin
of your still head Puerto Rico.

The business men who control
know nothing of the fine weather—
nor of themselves
Their windows are closed
and they no longer have hands
If they knew of their hands
and how good your body smells
They would encircle you
and kiss you all in the
greenness of your lomas-
Mayaquez legs so good
And Orocovis your belly button
I sit here in the middle of the
plaza in Cieba
Warming in the hottest fire
of las fiestas patronales
And I stare in the direction
Where I think is the closest
Mountain—
            For it seems that
from the top of the mountains—
Come voices.

Morena

If I found you in
Borinken
In a garden surrounded by rocks
I would slowly enter
And play with your hair

Like rhythm is your belly
It moves to this
Listen there is talk to this
la salsa de dios

As if the avenue
was the wet sand of the beach
Glide in memorial glances
Your eyes are like a strange
book
Walking in tune with flowers

In the garden of rocks
Some songs / some songs
So old for your eyes
For the tribe to grow
In the juice of your
belly.

african things

o the wonder man   rides his space ship/
                              brings his power through
many moons
              carries in soft blood   african spirits
dance & sing in my mother's house. in my cousin's house.
black as night can be/   what was Puerto Rican all about.
                                   all about the
indios & you better believe it the african things
                              black & shiny
grandmother speak to me & tell me of african things
                              how do latin
boo-ga-loo sound   like you
                    conga drums in the islands   you know
the traveling through many moons
                    dance & tell me black african things
i know you know.

Poem

Think with your body
And dance with your mind.

Loíza Aldea

Loíza
Who is there   in you took
a walk   Sandy walks
y Jose y Jane   in Loíza
the rain
The Coconut that had wings
of rum
In that bar-café   Sunday
night
Palm trees are the first
to wake in the mornings
and walk around the streets
Loíza—who was you

"who that in deep natural
  woods . . . who that walking
naked in the forest rain . . .
who that . . . if it's as sweet
as the dulce de coco then
come here we would like to
eat"
She came when she came in
dreams
When she came
Above her Flamboyant red feathers
She hears laughter and song
She hears all the salsa that
is played on her ground
They hit six drums with one hand
She knows all the Aldea

Lit up with la Fiesta de
Santiago   Lit up like natural
glow from the mangos hanging
from the trees
Horses dressed with gowns
Coconut faces parading
Mediania Baja
Tumba /unquinto from the night
If legs played drums
The body moves like the drum
Drum/in motion tumba   The song
jumps on the head—the head jumps
like the leg/sounds like the drum
drum   talk to body   tumba
Body talk for drum
fingers make it laugh   Body
come so close   Loíza   is the
wind you like to blow
Above the town your legs
unfold   Everywhere you
look carnaval   a sea of laughter
dancing   coming
The plaza is full
In brown sandals we walk
the walks   we stand to eat the
food   shirts are opened
Breeze Loíza you are soft and
warm
The waves
The red dresses
The pink and yellow
La plaza la plaza lit
The merry go round the smell

of shuffling bodies
Loíza
Loíza Aldea
On fire
Over there where fruits dance
into your mouth
& love comes gently
We sit till the morning
The wind blows festive sleep
Loíza you are always there
Silent with your African swing
Salsasa.

Aguadilla

We went to the house
Across the nation
The last people who went spoke of
the house being invisible from the
inside
Feel the house like the water
of Aguadilla
See the house like the walk of the
children in uniforms to school
We took the road by the ocean
We stopped into everything
By the stand where they sell cold
coconuts
The fried fish stand

☆

We can go into the house and not go

☆

It is a thousand years old
We practice Mambo till early morning

"You think it will rain before we get
to the banana trees?"

☆

It stayed dry in Aguadilla
Chopping bananas all afternoon

☆

The stove was burning
And the soft yellow smell of banana

☆

And so the skin of a conga

also burns
Seven drums and three maracas
One quiro
14 bodies two blocks from the beach

☆

Throwing rocks at mango trees
they fall into our hands

☆

The weekend began on Thursday
and ended Monday night

☆

The roosters are not given food
so they can grow mad and fight
In the round circle of the sport
Where the dollars fly into the
pockets of the strong

☆

The house is light pink
Two floors and many windows
From the house we move to Mayaguez
The drums are sticking out of the
trunk
Drink beer under the sun
Sun melts the cans

☆

The road back to Aguadilla
We meet up with caballeros
on horses

☆

The house is still there
We see it from far
Forming from a small dot
We make out the pink sticking out

from all the greenness
Our caravan moves fast   including the
laughter
Including the fruits taken from the
lonely trees
From the house we hear the sea
Yemaya is blue and white
her song is deep within

☆

We carry the drums on our backs
We go to the edge of the ocean
just where the water reaches
We turn around to look for the house
But it is not there
All we see is green rhythm coming
to eat us
Aguadilla   Sat.
                Sun.   Summer   1971

To The Spirit Of Carlos Gardel

Songs of tears
Gallons of rum to
drown your fears
Generation of madness
Millions of children
were born that year
They are my fathers
My mothers
Listening now
To the old 78's
Streams of thought
Invade the faces
They open
And Carlos Gardel
Sways out
With his tango
His tango
That kept everybody
In love.

Séis Amarrao

Slow afternoon of Caguas
The tall clock of the plaza

The public cars united like
a string   Along the green of
trees   Water fountains   in the
hottest afternoons

This town holds my grandmother
In her ancient dreams
Sewing dresses and cooking food
Somewhere in a quiet street
within

Our embrace is tears
Here I am to see you

As I said I would
Quiet in the night of memories
Quiet in the valley over the mountain
Quiet like the lips of Caquax.

Sabroso

I feel joy when I press against
the window and look into
the inside of what you are
Blue flowered walls
White Flamingos
Miniature elephants walk in your
Living room
It feels Sabrosisimo
to me glued to you
any Sunday afternoon of your
orangehead spanish tales
Daniel Santos story boleros
"why did she go and where
   is she now"
Pink bedroom and Jesus
Christ hangs wooden on
the wall
Outlined around each doorway
painted purple
The last supper in maroon
cloth on the wide living room
wall   Across from the little
flying silver birds
Below the fish made of
glass swim waterless on the
coffee table
Inside of what you are
Breathing 7,000 years of memories
Older than the walls
The colors of your mind

come out of your ears
Here pressed against the
window
I watch the show that falls
Sabrosisimo
Sabor.

The Man Who Came To The Last Floor

There was a Puerto Rican man who
came to New York
He came with a whole shopping bag
full of seeds strange to the big
city
He came and it was morning
and though many people thought the
sun was out this man wondered:
"Where is it"
"Y el sol donde esta" he asked
himself
He went to one of the neighborhoods
and searched for an apartment
He found one in the large somewhere
of New York
with a window overlooking a busy avenue
It was the kind of somewhere that is
usually elevatorless
Somewhere near wall/less
stairless
But this man enjoyed the wide space
of the room with the window that
overlooked the avenue
There was plenty of space
looking out of the window
There is a direct path to heaven
he thought
A wideness in front of the living
room
It was the sixth floor so he lived

on top of everybody in the building
The last floor of the mountain
He took to staring out of his sixth
floor window
He was a familiar sight every day
From his window he saw legs that
walked all day
Short and skinny fat legs
Legs that belonged to many people
Legs that walk embraced with nylon socks
Legs that ride bareback
Legs that were swifter than others
Legs that were always hiding
Legs that always had to turn around
and look at the horizon
Legs that were just legs against
the grey of the cement
People with no legs
He saw everything hanging out
from his room
Big city anywhere and his smile
was as wide as the space in front of him

One day his dreams were invaded by spirits
People just saw him change
Change the way rice changes when it is
sitting on top of fire
All kinds of things started to happen
at the top of the mountain
Apartamento number 32
All kinds of smells started to come out
of apartamento number 32
All kinds of visitors started to come

to apartamento number 32
Wild looking ladies showed up
with large earrings and bracelets
that jingled throughout the hallways
The neighborhood became rich in legend
One could write an encyclopedia if one
collected the rumors
But nothing bothered this man who was
on top of everybody's heads
He woke one day and put the shopping bag
full of seeds that he brought from the island
near the window
He said "para que aproveche el fresco"
So that it can enjoy the fresh air
He left it there for a day
Taking air
Fresh air
Grey air
Wet air
The avenue air
The blue legs air
The teen-agers who walked below
Their air
With their black hats with the red
bandana around them full of cocaine
That air
The heroin in the young girls that
moved slowly toward their local
high school
All the air from the outside
The shopping bag stood by the window
inhaling
Police air

Bus air
Car wind
Gringo air
Big mountain city air anywhere
That day this man from Puerto Rico
had his three radios on at the same time
Music coming from anywhere
Each station was different
Music from anywhere everywhere

The following day the famous
outline of the man's head once again showed
up on the sixth floor window
This day he fell into song
and his head was in motion
No one recalls exactly at what point
in the song he started flinging the
seeds of tropical fruits down to
the earth
Down to the avenue of somewhere big
city
But no one knew what he was doing
So all the folks just smiled
"El hombre esta bien loco, algo le
cogio la cabeza"
The man is really crazy
something has taken his head
He began to throw out the last of the
Mango seeds
A policeman was walking down the avenue
and all of a sudden took off his hat
A mango seed landed nicely into his
curly hair
It somehow sailed into the man's

scalp
Deep into the grease of his curls
No one saw it
And the policeman didn't feel it
He put his hat on and walked away
The man from Puerto Rico
was singing another pretty song
His eyes were closed and his head waved.

Two weeks later the policeman felt
a bump coming out of his head
"Holy shit" he woke up telling his wife
one day
"this bump is getting so big I can't
put my hat on my head"
He took a day off and went to see his
doctor about his growing bump
The doctor looked at it and said
it'll go away
The bump didn't go away
It went toward the sky
getting bigger each day
It began to take hold of his whole head
Every time he tried to comb his hair
all his hair would fall to the comb
One morning when the sun was really hot
his wife noticed a green leaf sticking
out from the tip of his bump
Another month passed and more and more
leaves started to show on this man's head

The highest leaf was now two feet above
his forehead
Surely he was going crazy he thought
He could not go to work with a mango
tree growing out of his head
It soon got to be five feet tall
and beautifully green
He had to sleep in the living room
His bedroom could no longer contain him
Weeks later a young mango showed up
hanging from a newly formed branch
"Now look at this" he told his wife
He had to drink a lot of water or he'd
get severe headaches
The more water he drank the bigger
the mango tree flourished over his head
The people of the somewhere city heard
about it in the evening news and there was
a line of thousands ringed around his
home
They all wanted to see the man who
had an exotic mango tree growing from
his skull
And there was nothing that could be done.

Everyone was surprised when they
saw the man who lived at the top of
the mountain come down with his shopping
bag and all his luggage
He told a few of his friends that
he was going back to Puerto Rico
When they asked him why he was going back
He told them that he didn't remember
ever leaving

He said that his wife and children
were there waiting for him
The other day he noticed that he was
not on his island he said
almost singing
He danced toward the famous corner
and waved down a taxi
"El Aire port" he said
He was going to the clouds
To the island
At the airport he picked up a newspaper
and was reading an article about a mango
tree
At least that's what he could make out of
the English
Que cosa he said   Wao
Why write about a Mango tree
There're so many of them
and they are everywhere
They taste goooooood
Como eh.

ABOUT THE AUTHOR

VICTOR HERNÁNDEZ CRUZ was born in Aguas Buenas, Puerto Rico. His poems have appeared in numerous anthologies and magazines in this country and abroad. *Mainland* is his second book of poems; he is currently working on a novel.